PATHWAY INTO THE WALLS OF COLLEGE

The Complete Student's Guide to Selecting Your Ideal College

KEITH HARRIS

FOREWORD

One's success is said to be highly influenced by a variety of factors, including knowledge, abilities, tenacity, and determination, to mention a few. But did you know that deciding on the best educational setting also has a significant impact on how your future will be shaped?

This book is something you need to read right away if you're one of the millions of students who haven't picked which university or college to attend. Learn how to select a university based on many criteria to increase your chances of achieving the level of achievement you have been aspiring to.

CHAPTERS...

CHAPTER 1

Wonder Why You are Going to College

This is a basic inquiry, yet the response seldom is. Most secondary school understudies don't have any idea what they believe they should do when they grow up. Yet, recollect that you're picking a school, not a significant one. Choosing the best school is the same amount as a course of finding out about yourself for all intents and purposes about imminent schools. seek after graduation, however, you surely understand what your inclinations and you're great at. Pondering this will assist you with sorting out whether or not you're inclining towards human sciences or a specialized field. Self-reflection will likewise assist you with getting a grip on different elements.

Would you want to attend a big or small school? Far away or near and dear? expensive or affordable? As you ask yourself these questions, you'll begin to have your unique demands for advanced knowledge.

You can attempt to think that you're not quite ready for school yet. If you must return home for the year, make wise use of your time. In some cultures, understudies are expected to take a year off after finishing their secondary education to travel, work, or volunteer. You must make sure you spend your time wisely because this is not common in the United States. Therefore, you must make sure that the time you spend is put to good use. They will need to know how you handled your excess energy during your prime years when you finally apply to schools.

CHAPTER 2

Do I belong to a large or small college?

If..., a large college might be the best fit for you

You excel at moving forward on your own. You don't frequently need assistance from teachers, and in the unlikely event that you do, you are prepared to remember and look for it.
To regularly explore, you need a large selection of clubs, sports, and workouts.
You think that when you tell people where you go, they should immediately recognize the name of your school.
You must support your team during pivotal moments since you enjoy sports.
You're unsure of your major or you're pursuing a niche major that isn't offered at smaller universities.

You're more likely to go for what you want and understand that many other students are vying for the same opportunities.

When you graduate, you must have a sizable network of your graduating class.

Large gatherings inspire and excite you.

You wouldn't be concerned about being taught by colleagues instead of your teacher.

You can accept responsibility for regularly checking your academic planner to make sure you're on track for your major.

You are confident that you will be able to find your neighborhood to identify with so that you don't get lost in the crowd. You would want to avoid running across people you already know.

You believe that examination should be a major component of your learning. This can help you graduate from undergrad and enter graduate school.

You wouldn't worry about using public transportation or walking a short distance to class.

If..., a small college could be the best fit for you

You depend on educators for support and guidance. You have trouble recognizing when you need help, so you rely on your teachers to step in when you truly need them.

You don't mind that there are fewer options for clubs, games, and movements. (While there will undoubtedly be many at almost all institutions, you will simply find a larger selection and more specialized options at larger schools.) You feel as though your professors and classmates should be aware of who you are since you need to interact with them in a small class environment.

If nobody from outside your community had heard of your school, it doesn't matter.

You might avoid attending sporting events or you might prefer more subdued settings.

You are confident more modest institutions offer your major.

Less competition is required for open doors (grants, work concentrated on positions, and so on.).

Given that there is far less competition than there would be at a large institution, this can mean that you have access to more opportunities.

You need to be aware of your school's graduating class, therefore organization is more important.

Large crowds quickly overwhelm you and shove you aside.

You insist that the people carrying out all of the teachings should be your teachers.

You contend that your advisor should be familiar with you and keep up with your needs, giving you advice if you are lacking something or reminding you of the courses you wish to enroll in.

You think the whole school ought to feel like a neighborhood. You like bumping into familiar people and coworkers everywhere you go.

Your instructional plan doesn't necessarily need to include research (many small schools don't have research offices).
You need your general education classrooms, other grounds offices, and your apartment to be incredibly close to one other.

Look at these lists and try to decide which one best suits you. Try placing a star next to every statement that describes you; you might be surprised to see which section gets the most stars.

Consider any of these justifications that are indisputable to you. If you're completely decided on your major, the decision will be made for you even if you have more stars in the small school category yet your major is only offered at larger universities.

CHAPTER 3

How many colleges to apply for

Most admissions experts agree that students should submit applications to four to twelve colleges, depending on their budget for application fees. To assist you make sure you're submitting applications to a balanced mix of institutions, you may categorize schools into "reach," "target," and "safety" schools.

Nevertheless, some prospective students are very certain about the institution or university they want to enroll in and don't feel the nieed

to submit several applications. These students may opt to keep their application pool narrow, applying to a select few schools or perhaps just one, rather than forking over application fees to institutions they have no interest in attending.

According to conventional wisdom among counselors, the typical college-bound kid should submit applications to 6–8 institutions, including 2-3 reach colleges, 2-3 target colleges, and 2 safety schools. Reach schools are those where your chances of admission are slim (less than a 30% chance), target schools are those where you have a good chance of admission (between a 30% and 80% chance), and safety schools are those where you almost certainly will be admitted based on your credentials (more than an 80% chance).

I recently had a conversation with a friend whose kid had submitted applications to about 20 institutions, which is unreasonably high. In any case, the investment was profitable. Despite being turned down by several lower-ranked institutions, he ultimately succeeded in getting into one of his target schools (and by some higher-ranked ones as well).

In actuality, many pupils would gain from using this tactic. While I don't advise kids to submit applications to 20 different colleges, there is a definite advantage to doing so.

It's easy to understand why Admissions choices to colleges might vary widely. Typically, there is no exact formula for entering your top choice of university. Although most institutions make it clear that academic achievements are important, many also take into account a few additional factors, such as community participation, extracurricular activities, background, and character.
Recognize, however, that by submitting fewer applications, you run a larger danger of having your applications for all universities denied.

CHAPTER 4

Create a list of colleges

Create a list of institutions that appeal to you early on in the process by sitting down with your parents, legal guardians, or another trusted adult, such as your guidance counselor at school. Public and private schools, both in-state and out-of-county, may be on this list. Before you make a decision, you should take into account a range of experiences and consequences. This list needs to contain four to

twelve universities, all of which ought to have majors that fit your interests and career objectives. Try to have more than one first pick if you want the college search process to be less depressing. Making sure that each institution on your teen's list is a good fit can help her feel less anxious (and maybe disappointed) when the college acceptance letters start to arrive. Teenagers sometimes become obsessed with the concept of attending a college after hearing about it for some reason, whether it be a sports title, a well-known alum, or the fact that someone in their family or close group of friends attended there. However, urge your youngster to approach the search from an open position.

CHAPTER 5

Tour College Campuses

Since students now visit a large number of universities, open days have surpassed the universities in importance. They used to only visit two or three places, but now they go to six or seven. Even there are occasions where students repeatedly attend the same university, such as when hunting for their first house as newlyweds. The open days are now handled with greater professionalism. They have already

deconstructed, with colleges considering each "experience" point, beginning with arrival,

moving on to parking, and meeting the ambassador guides, with the entire team having received thorough training on potential questions

and similar. It may be exciting to visit institutions during open days, and to make the most out of this exciting experience, there are things that you need to do for it to be a great day.

- Do not overlook the postcode. This thing is very easy to do but unfortunately, many tend to forget it, thus ruining their experience
- Even if you might have better antennas if you go to the open day alone, it might still be helpful to have another pair of vigilant eyes to scan the surroundings and determine whether they would be good for you or not
- Do you feel comfortable in the area?
- Open days isn't just about the course you've chosen because these details may be simply discovered online. These incidents mostly concern whether or

whether you can stay and dwell in one area for a long time.

- how it feels to be there while it's heavy raining or when the sun is very hot up there in the sky.
- How does the lodging look? Is it allotted correctly?

The internet is still a fantastic resource for learning about degree programs, investigating colleges and institutions, and getting to know professors and staff. However, visiting the campus in person offers more insight than simply browsing a school's website.

You and your family may learn more about the school's culture, ask questions, dine in the cafeteria, and look at on-campus housing by touring college campuses. Check to see whether you can easily envision yourself going.

CHAPTER 6

Comparing financial aid offers

Different universities offer financial aid packages that can significantly help in lowering the overall cost of attending college in order to

assist their students in completing their studies without the need to be burdened by all the school expenses.

The greatest option you have when looking for a school that provides financial help for its students is to visit their official website to find out more about its criteria.

Many students are currently supported by these packages, and the majority of them were able to do so by simply meeting the requirements established by the schools.

While the total cost of attending college is a very important aspect.

Being a financially savvy student is essential while looking for a university. It goes without saying that you should never enroll in a program that will put you in serious debt before you even graduate. Why will you select a reasonably priced university? . To know if your chosen university is something that you can afford, you should start by calculating your education's actual cost. Try to add up in advance all the expenses that you will have, like tuition, school, fees, living expenses and books

before you factor in all the available financial aid, like grants, scholarship, student loans and work-study.

A greater financial assistance package can be the deciding factor when choosing a school if you want to graduate with little or no debt. You can better understand your actual out-of-pocket expenses by comparing annual charges and analyzing financial assistance award letters.

CHAPTER 7

What to Look for in a College: 6 Things to Take Into Account

The decision of which institution to attend is a significant one, and students should carefully consider all of their alternatives before deciding on one. While each student has unique requirements and interests, everyone should take the following considerations into account while making a choice.

1. Location in Space

For many students, location is one of the most important considerations when selecting a college. You may be eligible for in-state tuition if you choose to continue your education at a public university in your home state, which might result in significant financial savings for you.

Since automobile journeys are typically less expensive than the flight, you may also reduce your travel expenses. Think about whether you

would want to live in a small town, a large metropolis, or somewhere in between.
Small college towns can provide a more personal feeling of community that allows you to forge close bonds with classmates and lecturers. Contrarily, schools in big cities might provide you access to more social and cultural events, as well as internships at significant businesses and nonprofits.

2. Academic Fields of Study
Make sure any school you are thinking about has a major that fits with your academic route if you already have a clear idea of it. For instance, students who are certain they want to major in art history should not give colleges that do not offer this degree a meaningful consideration.
On the other hand, students who are still unsure of their academic objectives might want to think about picking a college that offers a wide range of majors.

3. Academic Excellence

No school can provide the top programs in every subject of study, despite what its marketing team may like you to think. Looking at BestColleges' rankings might help you gauge a college's general academic standing and reputation before enrolling.

The college's accreditation should then be verified. Next, check to discover if certain academic departments have the necessary accreditation. For instance, you'll probably want a school that has been approved by a relevant professional organization if you intend to pursue a business administration degree.

If the faculty in your target department has gotten any honors or recognition for any ground-breaking publications or discoveries, you may use that information to estimate their career and research accomplishments.

4. Size of School

There are all different sizes of schools and universities, from little liberal arts institutions with fewer than 1,000 students to massive state

universities with more than 50,000 students enrolled each year.

Smaller institutions might not offer as many programs, but they frequently offer specialized degrees, including majors that students choose themselves, and experiential learning opportunities. Smaller class numbers at small universities may also make it easier for you to get one-on-one assistance from professors and academic counselors.

Because they may benefit from the variety of courses, extracurricular activities, and professional resources available at large colleges, students with specific interests and aspirations often succeed there. Larger institutions frequently have well-stocked libraries, cutting-edge research labs, and nationally renowned athletic programs

5. Total Price

You'll frequently be eligible for cheaper tuition costs if you select a public university close to your home.

The average tuition and fees for in-state students attending a four-year public university were $9,349 in 2019–20, while out-of-state students paid $27,023, according to the National Center for Education Statistics. Private institutions charged students an average of $32,769 in tuition and fees in 2019–20, regardless of residence status. When estimating the entire cost of attendance, you must also account for accommodation and board, transportation, books and supplies, and any supplemental student expenses. The finest universities provide competitive financial assistance programs and reasonable tuition rates. Consult an academic counselor to learn more about the loans, grants, scholarships, and work-study programs that your chosen school offers.

6. The Campus Setting

When selecting a college, it's critical to take the campus environment into account because personal and professional development also takes place outside of the classroom. Depending on your interests, you might want to investigate colleges that place a high priority on Greek life or have a thriving art scene.

Consider colleges with famous athletic teams if you enjoy the spirit of sports camaraderie so you may attend games and other social activities. Similar to this, you can meet new people through recreational and competitive activities at colleges with active intramural sports clubs.

Consider enrolling in a research university that has been accredited by the Carnegie Foundation if academic achievement is your major priority. These universities devote a significant amount of funding to professor and student research initiatives.

CHAPTER 8

Considering You're Still Uncertain

If you've done your research and visited a few schools but still can't come to the conclusion that common decency applies to you, a good option is to choose a large school with smaller branch grounds. So, you may start at any kind of grounds you decide you'd like and, if you find yourself becoming discouraged there, you can go to bigger or smaller grounds.

Going to a smaller branch campus of a larger university can also provide you with the finest results. You will receive many of the benefits of a large university, such as a sizable graduated class organization and name recognition, but you will do so on a smaller campus.

Another option is to start at one type of institution and just enroll in general education (gen ed) courses that will transfer to other schools. If you take general education classes for a short time at a less expensive school and then transfer to your dream school for the remainder of your education, this could also be a way to save some money.

It can seem like you're stuck there once things start going at school or in a relationship, and that moving forward is your only real option. If you start at one school and discover that you are hopeless and that you have chosen an inappropriate course of action, you won't stay there for velong. If it makes you happy and indicates that you are better prepared to organize the rest of your life, an extra little while is worth the effort even if it means it

takes you a little longer to finish school. Your speculative profit is a crucial last factor to take into account if you're on the fence. With a degree from a large, prestigious university, are you certain to find employment in a lucrative field? Actually, no.

The universities with the highest graduate salaries are listed in PayScale's College Salary Report, and both small and large universities are represented.

www.ingramcontent.com/pod-product-compliance
Lightning Source LLC
LaVergne TN
LVHW052113160826
845678LV00015B/3535

9798351705385